A little boy and his mother and father live in a lighthouse. If you want to go to see them, how do you get there?

The King is coming to his palace in India. The guards are waiting for him. How will he come?

Six people have climbed a mountain. They are hot and tired, but they want to go on to the top of a still higher mountain. How will they get there?

It is very hot in the desert. A lady and a gentleman want to go to see the Sphinx and the Pyramids. They look at them in the distance and wonder how they will get there.

There is treasure lying at the bottom of the sea. Who will find it, and how will they get there?

An Eskimo boy and his mother are waiting for Father to come home so that they can make some reindeer stew. How will Father come?

Two cowboys on a ranch want to go across the plains to another ranch miles away. The boy and his dog know how they will get there, do you?

Two men sit in a little boat near the shore of an island. The boat is too small to get across the sea but one of the men must go. How will he do it?

The road stretches ahead. How will this little man get to the end of it?

Published by
Chatto & Windus Ltd.
40 William IV Street
London WC2N 4DF

Text and illustrations © H. A. Rey 1957

First published 1957
Seventh impression 1976

All rights reserved
ISBN 0 7011 0188 1

Printed by
Lawrence-Allen Ltd.
London and Weston-super-Mare